VENICE
together

DISTRIBUITED BY:

EDITIONS ZERELLA - VENICE

S. MARCO 3576 - Telephone: 041/5205797

A BRIEF HISTORY

Osella. *Gold and silver coins from Venice's Zecca or mint.*

THE ORIGINS OF VENICE

If the remote, legend-shrouded dates handed down to us by the history books are to be believed, the seeds of Venice began to sprout amid the desolate shoals and marshlands about 450 AD. Of the city and state that would come to be renowned as a sea power under the title «Serenissima Repubblica Marinara di San Marco e La Dominante», the first inhabitants, seeking refuge in the islands of the lagoon from the nearby coastal towns and villages laid waste by Attila, were survivors; their rude huts, the first dwellings.

Other barbarian invasions — the Visigoths, Ostrogoths and Lango-bards — were to follow, bringing a steady influx of new settlers. In time, there developed on the larger islands politically and economically orga-nised settlements such as Chioggia, Torcello, Burano and Malamocco, with the latter becoming

Dates, Events and People. By the late 7th century AD, the grandchildren of those who had sought refuge in the lagoon from Attila, the Visi-goths and other barbarian tribes had fashioned viable and thriving settlements through undaunt-ing courage and hard work. And the Byzantine Empire, from its capital at Ravenna on the Adriat-ic, was quick to take notice. It seizes the Lagoon and appoints Paoluccio Anafesto (697), consid-ered Venice's first Doge (Dux, leader in Latin), to govern.

Fishing, trade, salt-works, and fruit and veg-etable growing (then as now the oldest of the la-goon's industries) are developed. As the decades pass, the inhabitants begin forging a collective identity. It grows steadily and coalesces in 88 when the people of the lagoon cast off the yoke of Constantinople and gain their complete inde-pendence.

This was the climax to a series of politic struggles over the lagoon between Byzantines and Franks. In 810 AD, Charlemagne's son, Pep-in, seized the capital Malamocco (Metamacus) forcing the population to take refuge in the safer, centrally located settlement on the island called Rialto. By the Pax Nicefori Treaty in 811, the By-zantines regain «caretaker» status over the La-goon, pitting them against the aspirations of free-dom and political independence of the Rialto's in-habitants.

This epoch also sees the construction of the Doge's Palazzo Ducale, a tower-appointed for-tress facing the sea and heralding the glorious era of the «Partecipazi» Doges. The bishop of the La-goon is installed at Olivolo (San Pietro di Castello) to represent the Church and the religious faith of the people.

829. Buono di Malamocco and Rustico di Tor-cello, two merchants (the Rialto's trade links al-ready stretch to the Levant), steal the body of St Mark the Evangelist at Alexandria, Egypt, hidden under layers of crated pork (untouchable under Islamic law so unexamined by the «customs» agents) and bring it back to the Lagoon. St Mark is proclaimed the city's patron (replacing St Theo-dore, called «Todaro» by the Venetians).

10th Century. The «Partecipazi» are suc-

2

e «capital» of the la-
oon communities. It is
o exaggeration to say
urvival was their grea-
st accomplishment.

They were continually
reatened by attack
om land and, with pi-
ates running the
straits» linking the
ackwaters of the la-
oon with the Adriatic
ea, from the sea. But
e islanders tenacious-
· held their ground. Fi-
ally, where once sea
ulls reigned unchal-
nged soaring aloft with
nly the sky above and
e water dotted by
pecks of marshland de-
erted save for their
ests below, these set-
ers emerged from the
long night» of fear and
ncertainty. They were
ore than mere surviv-
rs. They were the foun-
ers standing in the
awn of what was to be-
ome a glorious new or-
er of human endea-
our.

e Doge's «Corno». *The*
p worn by the Venetian
oges as a symbol of their
cal authority.

*The flag of the galleass which belonged to Doge Domeni-
co Contarini (XVII century).*

ceeded by the Candiano and Orseolo Doges. The
Venetian trade empire expands on the mainland
and seaward to include the Adriatic's eastern
shore (Capodistria in Yugoslavia pays its first tribute to Rialto Venice in 932), the Aegean and numerous Levantine ports. The political strife between Eastern and Western Empires in this period is also felt in Venice. During a revolt, Doge Pietro Candiano IV is killed and the Palazzo Ducale
along with neighbouring districts are burned.
Internicine struggles among families and factions
continue under Doge (later saint) Pietro Orseolo I.
Internal peace is restored by Doge Pietro Orseolo
II, and the rise of Venice as a major power begins
with her conquest of Dalmatia in the year 1000 on
Ascension Day (still celebrated as the «Festa della Sensa»).

The early years of the 11th century witness the
first display of Venice's naval might. Allied with
Byzantium, it defeats the Saracens and drives
them from Bari. The city on the Rialto has come of
age — as a political and military peer of Byzantium
and as a European power broker. Although chal-
lenged by the Normans of Robert Guiscard later in
this century, Venice emerges astutely unscathed,
all the while expanding its commercial enter-
prises at the expense of Constantinople.

As its international stature changed, so did its
internal one. Architecturally. The huts had given
way to town houses and palazzi, the canals were

3

VENICE AND ITS ARCHITECTURE

Even a cursory first glance will tell you Venice is a city of many architectural styles. Each one represents a distinct period yet bears inherent formal idiosyncrasies and subtle quirks as to give it a distinctive Venetian flair or originality. The five main styles you will encounter are the Byzantine, Romanesque, Gothic, Renaissance and Baroque.

The Byzantine. Briefly put, what makes this style unmistakable are such traits as vastly imposing buildings that stress ornate, detailed eastern decorative motifs and the picturesque massing of elements with various forms of arches culminating in vaulted domes or cupolas. For example, stilted arches that are round, horseshoe-

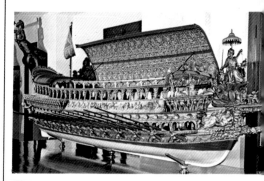

Bucintoro. *The golden galley used from the 13th century on by the Doge and his court when presiding over the Republic of St Mark's solemn ceremonies. The most famous of these was the «nuptial rite» wedding the «Serenissima» to the Adriatic.*

solidly shored up and the sand banks no longer bulged with the silt and water from the mainland streams and rivers. Though not yet the incomparable Venice we are accustomed to, it is a city.

The Crusades. «Venetians first, then christians». This aptly captures Venice's single-minded pursuit of trade and new markets. Its initial indifference to the Crusades, however, is later changed to intervention by two developments. The realisation that its own disinterest threatens to undermine its position **vis à vis** the rival maritime republics of Genoa and Pisa and, above all, the intimidatory tactics of the Byzantine Emperor Commenus. In an effort to regain control of the Italian Adriatic territories, he has all Venetian merchants within the empire arrested. Doge Vitale Michiel responds by sending an expeditionary force against him. Although the Venetians suffer a humiliating defeat, the setback proved a minor one. The city continues to play a leading role in European politics, even hosting the conference leading to the 1177 Peace of Venice, the armistice signed by Pope Alexander III, Frederick I Barbarossa, the Lombard League and Norman Sicily.

The 4th Crusade. In return for its participation, Venice receives armed support in recapturing Zara in Dalmatia, which had rebelled against it with the aid of the Hungarians. This is the Crusade of Enrico Dandolo, the famous blind Doge who di-

aped or four-pointed; orn-
e capitals with acanthus
f motif; carefully selected,
loured marble; highly de-
rative mosaics covering
lls and floors. This style
edominated in Venice from
e 6th to the 12th centuries,
d is best exemplified in the
agnificent St Mark's Basili-

e **Romanesque.** It is
sily identifiable by its
inted vault or arch and
ck bearing walls that
aracterise buildings of the
th and 13th centuries. In
nice this style is basically
sub-order of the Byzantine
d prelude to the Gothic.

e **Gothic.** A term origin-
y coined by Italian Ren-
ssance artists to indicate
erogatively all medieval Eu-
pean art from the 12th to
th centuries, it came to de-
te in time an exact histori-
l style free of any negative
nnotations. It is the archi-
cture of the pointed arch,
e ribbed vault, pilaster-
rip and flying buttress. The
ildings are marked by ver-
alism, rising tall and slen-
er into the sky, symbols of
e religious solemnity and
nse of self-importance
at characterise the bour-
eoisie of North Europe's

rected the Crusader armies in the taking of Constantinople (1204). It also opened new ports to
Venice in Greece, Albania and Dalmatia and
brought under her control Candia and other Aegean islands. The Venetian galleys return laden
with the fabulous spoils of the Middle East, treasures destined for the Republic's patrician elite,
their sumptuous palazzi and the city's churches.
The 1200s are witness also to the fame of Marco
Polo. Merchant, traveller and narrator of his own
adventures, he spread the name of Venice to the
very heart of China.

The 13th and 14th centuries are the stage upon
which the incessant rivalry — «visceral antagon-
ism» — between Venice and Genoa is played out.
Although Genoa is finally defeated in the naval
battle of Chioggia, Venice's triumph is a bitter
one. She loses Dalmatia and part of her mainland
Veneto «territories» — the Trevigiana March, re-
taken in the early 1400s — by the Peace of Turin in
1381.

This reversal is shortlived. Venice soon adds
the mainland colonies of Padua, Vicenza, Verona
and all of Friuli as well as regaining control of Dalmatia on the other side of the Adriatic. Under
Doge Francesco Foscari (1423-57), the Republic
is engaged in a long series of land wars, made famous by the deeds of such renowned «condottie-
ri» or mercenaries as Carmagnola, Gattamelata
and Colleoni. Bergamo and Brescia also fall to the
banner of St Mark.

By this time, too, Venice had been forced onto
the defensive in the Aegean and Levant (since the
mid-1300s) by the Ottoman Turks. Either by reac-
tion to or as compensation for these losses, Venice pushed westward to the Po river, taking
Cremona, and northward to the Dolomites, the
Giulia Alps and Quarnaro in Italy, while in the eastern Mediterranean, it tries to reassert its power by
having Caterina Cornaro, «its» Queen of Cyprus,
«donate» the island to the Republic in 1489.

The onset of Venice's decline is, however, evi-
dent by the end of the 1400s. With the discovery of
the New World in the West, the Levant, and Venice, gradually lose their importance as centres of
power and trade. The changing political situation
in Europe is also against the Republic. The
emergence of the first nation states and her defeats at the hands of the Turks undermine Ve-

5

free cities or communes. In Venice the Gothic flourished from the 12th to the 15th centuries. The Palazzo Ducale, unique in both size and composition, is the city's finest example. In effect, this style blended so well with the natural environment that it soon took on quite original elements that can still be distinguished today.

6

The Renaissance. The term was coined in the 1800s to mean the cultural and artistic movement that originated and flourished in Italy from the 15th to the 16th centuries. It eschewed the Gothic and mystical tendencies of the Middle Ages so that it could revive (**rinascimento** means rebirth in Italian) and adapt classical forms to the demands of the time. Greek and Roman styles were propounded as examples of proportion and harmony of composition to be included in the new style. Cinquecento (1500s) architecture evolves a new concept of space — precisely defined, well ordered in its parts and stressed by the perfect harmony of the clear, sharp lines of its buildings.

Doge Sebastiano Venier, victor at Lepanto.

nice's stature and sap her vitality. In attempting to forestall destiny, she seizes the mainland cities of Rimini, Faenza, Urbino and Forlì only to find herself pitted against an array of foes — the League of Cambrai (1508), Pope Julian II, Spain, Mantua, Ferrara, Savoy, France and Germany. Even defeat brings no respite. France and Spain will remain at length implacable enemies, alternating in their roles as often as the changes in the political winds dictate.

The situation worsens as the Turks take Cyprus. And, despite the famous naval victory over the Turks at Lepanto in 1571 under the leadership of Doge Sebastiano Venier, «captain of the seas», Venice's political and military fortunes continue to slide. More Aegean islands fall, including Candia (1669). Even its capture of Morea under Morosini is to no avail as the Turks will retake it in 1715. Vain, too, are Venetian attempts to seize Tunis, Tripoli and Algiers along the Northaf

8

he Baroque. It follows he Renaissance and is noted for such stylistic qualities s the enthusiastic use of urving decorative motifs, alustrades, colonnades, iches, segmented pediments and complex spatial rrangements. The lines of iches and colonnades are ll too often broken by statues of exuberant forms and raping but lacking in psychological expressivity. The ast and imposing Basilica ella Salute is Venice's most nportant example.

Canaletto: Palazzo Ducale.

rican coast. Its fate is irrevocably sealed, and the valiant efforts of such leaders as Angelo Emo and Jacopo Nani cannot prevail against it.

The end comes with the advent of Napoleon Bonaparte in the late 1700s. Lodovico Manin, the last Doge, can muster neither the will nor the means to defend the «Serenissima». Thus, on the 12th of May 1797, the Republic of Venice surrenders its glory and independence.

The following century, marked by the events of 1848-49 and 1866, belongs to Italy's struggle for a national state. Today the city of the Doges and St Mark thrives on both the heritage of its past and its substantial role in modern Italian society.

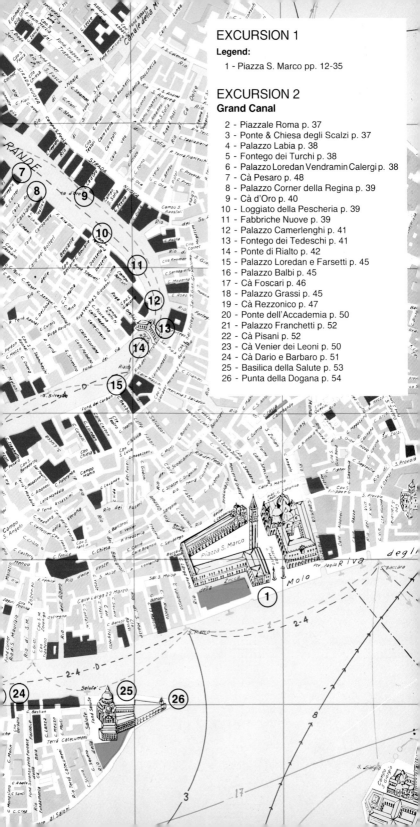

EXCURSION 1

Legend:

EXCURSION 2

Grand Canal

Excursion 1

PIAZZA SAN MARCO

Once off the boat or launch at St Mark's Calle Vallaresso, it's but a brief detour to Campo San Moisè and its Baroque church named after the saint with its 14th-century bell tower and brick steeple. From here, a short walk across the «salizzada» and you're under the arcade of the Ala Napoleonica with light-filled Piazza San Marco, Venice's open-air «salon», and the resplendent Basilica d'Oro (golden) before you.

Originally a grass field divided by the Batario canal, St Mark's Square (Piazza San Marco) has been called the world's «most beautiful sitting room». Here are the gold and marble lace-work of the Basilica and the four magnificent steeds of St Sophia that feign to gallop. There the Procuratie colonnades stretch the length of the sides where mean wood and brick houses once stood and, where the Piazza and the Piazzetta meet, rises the Campanile or bell tower with its finely wrought, rose-coloured Loggetta by Sansovino which offers the golden angel at its top to the sky. The arch of the Clock Tower acts as a doorway between the city proper and the resplendent

Geminiano. It was razed by Napoleon to make room for the new wing connecting the two Procuratie. The Piazza itself is a trapezoid, 175.70 metres long and 82 m wide on the Basilica side and 57 m wide on the opposite side. Until a few decades ago, the square was illuminated by its graceful «ferali» or cluster-light lanterns, unfortunately replaced by four rather common beam-hung lamps.

St Mark's Campanile. Erected over a thousand years ago, the Campanile or bell tower of St Mark's is as then the city's highest structure. In the days when it was used as a lighthouse for ships, the lagoon's waters almost reached up to it.

The exact date of its building is unknown. Some sources give the year 888 AD, while others prefer the span from 902-911 during the rule of Doge Pietro Tribuno. What is certain is that the work took many years. The tower itself was erected during the reign of Doge Tribuno Memmo, and the giant terracotta «flue» was completed in 1152 (Doge Domenico Morosini) under the direction of the brothers Pietro and Giovanni Basilio, the head craftsmen. The belfry was added later by Nicolò Barattieri and Bartolomeo Malfatto.

Following damage from lightning, fire and earthquake in subsequent years, Bartolomeo Bon from Bergamo, perhaps after the design by Giorgio Spavento, executed the new belfry, the attic storey and the pyramid-shaped spire topped by the revolving figure of the Archangel Gabriel in gold-plated copper («raised on high amidst a fanfare of trumpets and fifes», as Sanudo noted on 6th July 1513). The Campanile was completed to its full 98.6-metre height in October 1514.

On July 14th 1902 at 9:47 AM, the bell tower, weakened by age and the damage of centuries, col-

light of the boat basin, while from its summit the two Moors strike their bronze hammers at the procession of the hours. The Ala Napoleonica (Napoleonic Wing) brings the background into relief, while the foreground is punctuated by Alessandro Leopardi's three poles from which fly the flag of Italy and the banner of St Mark. And the Batario still flows silently beneath the square's flintstone paving.

Under the rule of Doge Sebastiano Ziani in the 12th century, the field was cleared, the Batario canal covered and buildings — which would give way in the Renaissance to the Old and New Procuratie we see today — erected. The first pavement had a herring-bone pattern and was laid in 1264; the present motif was designed by Andrea Tirali and completed in 1723. At the end of the square opposite the Basilica once stood the church of San

lapsed, causing an outcry that was heard around the world. «As it was, where it was». This was the decision of the city council on rebuilding the Campanile. With the aid of modern construction techniques, it was inaugurated on the feast day of St Mark in 1912.

From above, the Campanile offers a matchless panorama. Galileo even used its height to display Venice and its islands through his telescope's magnifying lens, and the Emperor Frederick III of Austria rode his horse up the 37 flights of stairs.

The Sansovino Loggetta. Erected by Sansovino in 1542 at the foot of St Mark's bell tower opposite the Palazzo Ducale's Porta di Carta, it occupies a site that originally was reserved for the wooden stalls rented to bakers and sundry merchants and later, in the 1400s, the Ridotto or noblemen's meeting hall. The Loggetta consists of a central 5-step base, a balcony with balustrade, a three-arch façade adorned with columns, and capped by an attic storey finely decorated with bas-reliefs and bordered by a balustrade. The niches house the bronze statues of Minerva, Apollo, Mercury

and Peace; the ornate marble work is everywhere.

Added in 1733, two magnificent bronze gates by Antonio Gai close off the gallery leading to the bell tower. The Loggetta itself, which had been left to deteriorate through neglect and exposure to salt spray, has recently been returned to its original splendour following restoration.

The Golden Basilica. Here perhaps, on the pale-hued sea bed of the Piazza and Piazzetta, driven by the fleeting storms of the Adriatic, the fabled queen of all oysters deposited and the city, that red and white coral madrepore whose roots and foundations lie in the sea, came to possess that most resplendent of pearls.

The cupolas — Ascension, Emanuel, Pentecost, St Leonard and St John — take their shimmering light from the sky and cast the sun's reflections through the echoing silent chords of exultant dawns and melancholy twilights.

The Byzantine spires — aedicules enshrining the statues of saints — and the decorations of the arcades are the sea's embroidery, the lace trim adorning the expanse of sky.

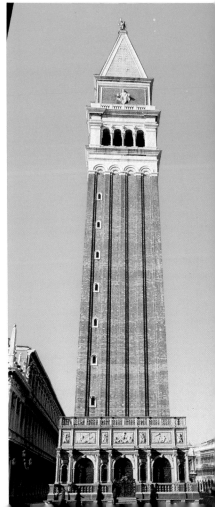

Within, the pearl is a golden hollow, the ark that holds from mosaic to mosaic, statue to statue and from stone to stone events of the Old and New Testaments.

The floors are carpets of inlaid marble, the altars abodes of the heart and soul. The ciborium is the focal point of man's faith and the Pala d'Oro (altar-piece) is the mirror of the God-given treasures humanity harbours within itself.

This is the pearl — the golden ark of St Mark, the Basilica of the Doges.

Originally of wood and stone, it served as the chapel of the Doges in the epoch when the Palazzo Ducale was still a moat-encircled square castle. In 828 the body of the Evangelist was laid here to rest,

and, following its destruction by fire, the church was rebuilt in the form of a Greek cross between 976-978.

And thus it was that throughout the centuries thereafter, age upon age bore witness to its basilica, each bestowing upon it according to its wealth at the behest of the foremost «caretaker» and devotee — the Doge. From Candiano Orseolo, Domenico Contarino, Selvo, Vitale Falier, Vitale Michiel II, Enrico and Andrea Dandolo, Antonio Venier and those who followed down to Foscari (for whom the large arch between the Basilica and the Palazzo Ducale is named), they gave, and with them the Serenissima's empire, the Orient, yielded its treasures to the splendour of St

One of the famous quadriga's gold-plated copper horses.

Mark's. Precious marbles, columns, capitals, statues, decorations, gold, jewels, architectural innovations and the quadriga's four golden steeds rampant in sculpted fury above the Piazza.

To visit the Basilica is to discover another world — a paradise of lights and shadows, of fretwork, voices from the past, devotion and the lure of the Orient. It is the final resting place of St Mark the Evangelist — the «half-naked boy» awakened by the clamor of Caiphas' soldiers at Judas' betrayal of his Master who saw the saddened face of Christ in the olive grove and vowed to bear him eternal witness. And, since 1807, it has been the seat of the Patriarchs of Venice and symbol of their dedication and faith.

Here are the five portals with their histories inlaid of gold, the bronze doors and their stands of pillars — all too subject to the ravages of time.

Enter... but with respect. For the outrages that have taken place under these sacred arches over the last few years by people from Italy and other countries in the form of impromptu camping-out and other abusive behaviour both collective and individual must be stopped, and these alienated and unhappy people must be prevented from continuing such acts. This is St Mark's Basilica — pearl of inimitable beauty that neither sea nor ocean will ever again create, heart of the Adriatic's madrepore that is Venice!.

The Quadriga. The name properly denotes the chariot of which the four gold-plated copper horses are the team. They once graced the Hippodrome of Constantinople until being removed as spoils of war by Doge Enrico Dandolo when he captured the city during the 4th

Crusade. A sublime example of Roman or Hellenic art, they were forcefully removed only once in the intervening centuries from the Basilica — by Napoleon in 1797 who wanted to display his plunder in Paris. In 1915 and 1940 they were taken down for safekeeping during the two world wars.

The four rampant horses outside the Basilica are copies of the originals which are now within. This was done following restoration of the four originals which had been badly damaged by pollution.

The Atrium. Filled with the brilliance of its gold mosaics and of the multi-hued marbles and groupings of columns, the atrium encloses the Basilica proper at the front and both sides. The closed right side houses the Zen chapel and the Baptistry. The open front and left side are composed of spans featuring cupolas, vaults, lunettes and niches — all covered with splendid mosaics depicting scenes from the Old Testament. The most important and best preserved are the Genesis cycle on the cupola opposite the side door of St Clement's chapel.

The pavement with its large circle-pattern marble mosaics features a large, bright red square having a diamond-shaped centre just before the main entrance. It marks the spot where the Emperor Frederick Barbarossa knelt when he met Pope Alexander III.

The central apse door is magnificent. Like St Peter's, St Clement's and St John's doors, it leads to the interior proper. In addition, it is graced by many fine columns and inlay work and has two small side entrances to the women's gallery, the terrace and St Mark's museum.

The Interior. Greek cross in plan, it has a central nave flanked by two aisles, galleries, a raised presbytery (under which is the crypt) and high altar (containing St Mark's body and featuring the Pala d'Oro), the apse with niches and the two small side chapels of Sts Peter and Clement. The five cupolas or domes — one at the centre of the cross — have windows at the base and pendentives on a double row of arches supported by corner piers.

Four thousand square metres of mosaics adorn the Basilica, bathing it in gleaming gold, and there are more than five hundred columns. Of the numerous capitals,

Basilica interior, transept left: A striking array of arches, domes, columns and women's galleries in the mosaics' golden glow.

The Ascension, the Basilica's central cupola or dome, the Double Ambo.

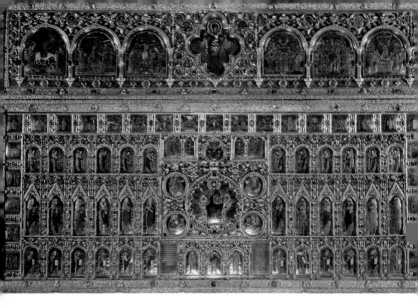

The Pala d'Oro. Eighty enamels, 1300 pearls, 400 garnets, 90 amethysts, 300 sapphires, 300 emeralds, 15 rubies, 75 balases, 4 topazes, and 2 cameos, all set in a gold plate measuring 3.48 by 1.40 metres adorn this magnificent altar-piece. A marvel of the Venetian goldsmith's art, it was fashioned in 1345 by Giampaolo Boninsegna who used enamels and precious stones from the original Pala dating to the period of Doge Pietro Orseolo I. Its shining aura befits the splendour of St Mark's altar.

The Nicopeia. Set in a double silver and enamel frame, this gold on wood painting of the Madonna and Child dates to the 9th century (the name is Greek for female spirit of victory). It came to symbolise protection for the Venetians who adorned it with jewels and ex voto. The Nicopeia is on the former altar of St John next to the small altar of St Paul to the left of the transept.

six are gold-plated in the form of a ram's head (11th century) along the nave and ten in the classical style adorned with acanthus leaves set against the transept's pillars.

The marble floor mosaics feature figures, symbols and geometric motifs. It is called «mare» or sea because it is undulated. This is due to the constant shifting of the ground and piles on which the basilica sits. The right aisle features a 12th-century Byzantine relief of a praying Madonna on St Clement's door, a holy-water stoup fashioned from the remains of a Roman fountain, and the tabernacle with a

Madonna and Child, called the «Madonna of the kiss» as in former times the faithful would kiss it. The entrance on the aisle's right leads to the Baptistry and Zen Chapel (1500).

The nave proper begins with the splendid Arch of Paradise followed by Tintoretto's mosaics, the fine Byzantine mosaic on the portal's

St Peter, Jesus praying on Mount Olive and the sleeping apostles. Detail of the superb 13th-century mosaic Jesus Praying in the Garden of Gethsemane covering the back wall of the Basilica's right aisle.

The Iconostasis.
A marble screen separating the sanctuary from the nave, the Iconostasis is an example of superb artistry by Jacobello and Pier Paolo delle Masegne in 1394.

The Crypt.
With its cross or groin vaults and many pillars, it still bears significant traces of the original Basilica.

lunette of «Christ in the act of benediction between Mary and St Mark», the splendid Arch of the Apocalypse, the four magnificent Byzantine angels on the Pentecost dome's pendentives, the four Evangelists on the Ascension dome's pendentives and the four marble angels of the transept.

The left aisle features an aedicule with Byzantine capitals protecting a crucifix on wood dated 1200 (miraculous bleeding is said to have occurred) that was part of the war spoils from Constantinople.

Divided into three small aisles, the transept on the left contains the Chapels of the Mascoli, St Isidore, the Nicopeia, and the marble altar of St Paul (1471). The right transept, also divided into three aisles, features the three rooms called the Treasury (containing objects of value, relics and icons from Constantinople), the magnificent Gothic rose window, the splendid St Leonard's dome, St James' marble altar (in the style of Pietro Lombardo) and the Chapel of the Holy Sacrament with its Baroque altar (designed by Contin in 1617) containing a relic of the True Cross. A lamp and angel on a nearby pillar commemorate the miraculous discovery of St Mark's body in 1094.

The Chapel of St Isidore. With its walls and tunnel or barrel vaults covered with ornate mosaics, it was built under Doge Andrea Dandolo in honour of the Saints of Chio whose body was brought to Venice in 1125.

The Chapel of the Mascoli. So called because it was the religious seat of the all-male (mascoli) Confraternities from 1618 on.

The Baptistry. Formed by combining several rooms of the Basilica's atrium, it was adorned and embellished with sculptures and mosaics in 1350 by Doge Andrea Dandolo whose tomb (by De Sanctis) is opposite the entrance. The Baptistry includes a hall with 13-th century mosaics depicting scenes from the childhood of Jesus and a spacious chapel. Above its altar is a mosaic portraying the crucified Christ flanked by the Madonna and three saints and being adored by the genuflecting Doge, his wife and the High Chancellor.

At the foot of the altar by the sarcophagus of Doge Giovanni Soranzo is the tombstone of Jacopo Sansovino, the artist who designed the marble baptismal font, its cover and bronze reliefs. The vaults,

domes and walls are decorated with mosaics of episodes from the lives of St John the Baptist, Christ, the Saints and Doctors of the Church.

The Clock Tower. The main tower is by Mauro Coducci and was built between 1496-99. The two side wings with their terraced upper stories, perhaps by Pietro Lombardo, were added later. In 1755, Giorgio Massari's terraces completed it, and the Renaissance Tower today stands in harmony with the Piazza.

On the square terrace atop the tower are the two Moors of dark, age-old bronze. Designed by Paolo Savin and cast by Ambrogio dalle Ancore, they strike the hours' passing on the great bell. Below them,

before a turquoise field studded with stars, the winged lion with his book of peace gazes out over the square and lagoon. The niche on the storey underneath houses a gold-plated copper Madonna and Child to whom homage is paid on Ascension Day (the Sensa) by an angel and the Magi in procession from one door to the other round the semi-circular balcony. The imposing clock face with the signs of the Zodiac, designed by the Ranieris of Reggio, crowns the arch forming the triumphal gateway between St Mark's Piazza and the Mercerie or shop district.

Marco and Tòdaro. High atop their capitals stand the statues of Venice's first patron saint, Teòdaro or Theodore, and what appears as the winged lion symbolising St Mark but which is actually a bronze chimera of Persian origin.

The Procuratie Vecchie. So called because they were originally the residences of the city's procurators or chief magistrates second only to the doge in authority, they stand on the site of earlier Byzantine-venetian style buildings that had been partly destroyed by fire. Begun about 1500, the Old Procuratie were designed by such famous artists and architects as Mauro Coducci, Guglielmo Bergamasco, Bartolomeo Bon and Jacopo Sansovino.

The «Pietra del Bando». Literally the stone of proclamation, this short, red porphyry column with white marble top slab is reputed to have been used as just that, i.e. dais from which public proclamations were read to the populace, in Acre, Syria, whence it was brought to Venice in the latter 1200s. It seems also to have served the Serenissima's authorities in the same capacity.

spoils along with the proclamation stone and pillars of Acre. It is set in the Basilica's outermost corner near Palazzo Ducale's Porta della Carta, and supposedly depicts as tetrarchs the four Roman emperors Diocletian, Maximian, Costantius and Galerius (but always popularly known as the four Moors).

The Acre Pillars. Standing on the left side of the Basilica, they were plundered from Acre following the defeat of the Genoese in 1256. Examples of Syriac-Egyptian art of the 5th and 6th centuries AD, the pillars are decorated with mysterious motifs and symbols attracting both scholars and the curious.

The Four Moors or Tetrarchs. Another work of red porphyry, this sculpture too comes from Acre (St John of Acre) in Syria and was part of the Venetian war

The Palazzo Ducale. Under Doge Angelo Partecipazio in the early 9th century AD, it was a castle-fortress of harsh unadorned walls, moat, towers, drawbridges and embrasures defending the newly formed city. With the Venetians' securing of the lagoon and mastery of the sea, the once rude building was transformed by refurbishment and additions (begun in 977 under Doge Pietro Orseolo I, ending in 1173) into the fabled palace of the Doges. A superb example of Gothic architecture on the grand scale, it is imposing yet luminous, its grandeur rendered airy by the stone lace-work, adornments, porticoes and loggias masking its massive bulk.

Further renovations and restoration (1483-1577 damaged by a series of fires) were undertaken from the early 1300s, culminating over the centuries in the palace of stylistic power and grace we see today.

Since its inception, many artists and architects have brought their skills and creative energies to bear in designing and embellishing the Palazzo Ducale. Baseggio, Calendario, the Bon brothers, Rizzo, Pietro Lombardo, Antonio Da Ponte

and Scarpagnino are the most renowned.

The building proper is a three-storey rectangle in plan with its north wall flush against the side of the Basilica, the church of the Doges until 1807. Of its three façades, the first on the Piazza and the second on the basin are both pure Gothic, while the third, rising from the water of the Rio di Palazzo, is unmistakably Renaissance in style. Enclosed by the walls of the Palazzo, yet bathed in light and chiaroscuro effects, is the inner courtyard.

The Scala dei Senatori, Scala dei Censori and Scala dello Scrutinio are the three stairways leading to the Palazzo's floors. A fourth, outside stairway connects the courtyard with the loggias.

A spectacular array of gold, marble and paintings, the Palazzo's great halls or «Sale» also have their own names — Sala del Piovego, dei Censori, della Cancelleria, degli Scarlatti, dello Scudo, Grimani, Erizzo, degli Stucchi, dei Filosofi, della Quarantia Civil Vecchia, della Quarantia Civil Nova, dell'Armeria, del Maggior Consiglio, dello Scrutinio, della Quarantia Criminale, delle Quattro Porte, del Collegio,

del Senato, del Consiglio dei Dieci, della Bussola, dei Tre Capi, degli Inquisitori di Stato. Austere yet appointed by the skilled hand of art are the Doge's apartments on the second floor. And, almost as a measure of human folly, there are the Serenissima's prisons—the «pozzi» or wells wedged into the Palazzo's very foundations and the «piombi» or leads cramped under the lead of the roof.

The Porta della Carta. Literally the Paper Door, it is the official entrance to Palazzo Ducale and was designed by the Bon brothers who executed it from 1438-42 in late Gothic style. The vertically paired canopied niches on either side contain the statues of the four virtues — Prudence, Justice, Fortitude and Temperance. The statues of the lion and Doge Francesco Foscari on the architrave were made by Ferrari in 1885 to replace the originals destroyed in 1797. Right above them is the three-light mullion window with its geometrical tracery.

Reputedly one of the world's most beautiful doors, its name is thought to derive either from the practice of posting the Republic's proclamations and decrees on it or because the scribes who drew up petitions were seated nearby.

The Cortile dei Dogi. A must for any visitor, the Doges' Courtyard is surrounded by colonnades and loggias, including the arcade, gallery and Arch named for Doge Francesco Foscari and built about 1470. The architectural styles vary greatly, and the Venétian predilection for «art in stone» culminates in the Arco Foscari (Foscari Arch) itself, with its finely wrought large and small columns, niches, capitals, statues and spires. The bronzes of Adam and Eve are especially noteworthy. Next to the Foscari Arch climbs the superb stairway called the «Scala dei Giganti» or Giants, and in the corner beyond it, above the small courtyard called the «Cortiletto dei Senatori» (senators) rises the red ridge of the Basilica.

Embellished by the two «vere» or well-heads, the courtyard features a pavement with white marble strip motifs similar to those of the Piazza and Piazzetta. The courtyard can be entered either by the Porta della Carta in St Mark's Square or by the Porta del Frumento (Wheat Door) facing the Molo (quay).

The Staircase of the Giants. A late 15th-century work by Rizzo, it is the only one of the four stairways to the loggia storey that leads outside, into the courtyard. Monumental, ornate with friezes and bas-reliefs, it features the dominating statues of Mars and Neptune sculpted by Sansovino about 1554 at its head. Between these two mythological figures and beneath the Lion of St Mark over the gallery's arch on the terrace, the Doges were once invested with the symbols of office.

The Scala D'Oro. The name, meaning golden stairway, comes from Alessandro Vittoria's gold-leaf stucco-work framing the frescos by Battista Franco. An open entrance flanked by Tiziano Aspetti's 16th-century statues of Hercules and Atlas in the east gallery leads to it. The Scala d'Oro appears to have been designed by Sansovino, though completed in 1559 by Scarpagnino.

The Sala dello Scudo. The Shield Room, so called because it displayed the Doge's coat-of-arms, was used as the official anteroom. The crest on display is in fact that of Ludovico Manin, the Republic's last Doge. The room's allegorical works and decorations are by Giustino Mescardi and date to the late 1700s. Also on display are two period globes.

The Sala dello Scrutinio. This is the room where the votes were cast and counted in the election of the doges and the city's highest magistrates (whence its name). It was rebuilt by Antonio Da Ponte in 1577 after being gutted by fire.

It features a triumphal arch to Peleponnesiacus on the rear wall as well as celebrated paintings by Tintoretto, Andrea Vicentino, Aliense, Sebastiano Ricci, Bellotto,

Liberi and Jacopo Palma il Gio-vane's (the younger) famous **Last Judgement** (Giudizio Universale). Above the cornice about the entire room are the portraits of the last 42 doges.

The ornate segmented ceiling with its splendid gilt frames features scenes depicting famous battles and episodes from Venice's history. The works are by various artists.

The Sala del Collegio. Literally the college room, this is where the doge convened his counsellors, the highest representatives of government, to discuss affairs of state and received ambassadors and nuncios. Almost destroyed by fire in 1574, it was refurbished by Andrea Da Ponte after designs by Andrea Palladio and Giovanni Antonio de Rusconi to its present state.

Palazzo delle Prigioni. This imposing building with its classical lines was built on the Riva degli Schiavoni between the late 1500s and early 1600s. The project architects were G.A. Rusconi, under whom work began, Antonio Da Ponte who took over in the middle stages, and Antonio and Tommaso Contino who completed it. An exemplary spaciousness is achieved by the square-columned arcade at street level.

Three rooms on the upper floor were once occupied by the «Signori della Notte», the magistrates charged with the night watch: prisoners, whence its name, were held in cells. Today this Palazzo is used as the site of art shows (held both inside and in the large courtyard), concerts, conferences and other social events.

The Ponte dei Sospiri. A famous reference point for visitors as it connects Palazzo Ducale to the Palazzo delle Prigioni (prisons), it is called the Bridge of Sighs because prisoners had to cross it on their way to trial or, condemned, back to the gloom of their cells. The bridge is of white Istrian stone in a Baroque style moderated by simplified lines and was designed by Antonio Contino in the 1600s under Doge Marino Grimani.

Conc. S.M.A. n. 447 del 17-7-72

Excursion 2

(map pp. 10-11)

THE GRAND CANAL

Piazzale Roma and Santa Lucia Railway Station are the gateways to Venice — tourists, scholars, travellers and people who are simply Venice lovers pass through these portals.

From them, you can slowly get a feel for the city by meeting it on its own terms — leisurely boating along the Grand Canal to the very heart of the city, turning as you go to see the light reflecting off St Mark's Basin, to catch a glimpse of the Lido that divides the lagoon from the open sea. Small steamers, regular city «bus» boats, the launch taxis or, if you're inclined towards the poetic, a gondola are always ready and waiting to take you.

Piazzale Roma. This is the plaza district, differing from insular Venice as it is almost «mainland» being the terminal point for connections between the mainland and the lagoon's city. It is here that roadways, bus and coach stations, car parks and garages converge. Here the greenery of the gardens and the boat and launch landings give way to water, and beyond to Venice. One is immediately drawn to this extraordinary city by the curious and picturesque sight of the four connected bridges spanning the Burchielle and Nuovo Rios (three are centuries-old and of stone and one is wooden of more recent date).

The Ponte degli Scalzi. A white marble arch connecting the banks of the Grand Canal by the Santa Lucia railway station, it was built in 1933 from plans by the architect Miozzi to replace an unsightly metal bridge erected during the Austrian occupation. To the right is the Church of Santa Maria di Nazareth (called the «barefoot» St Mary whence the term «scalzi») designed by Longhena with its Baroque façade the work of Sardi. The tomb of Ludovico Manin, the last of the doges, is in this church.

Palazzo Labia. This 18th-century Palazzo is an example of the architectural splendour the privileged Venetians demanded of their homes. It was first restored by its previous owner, Don Carlos Besteigui, and more recently by the current one, RAI, the Italian State TV and Radio network.

Fontego dei Turchi. The «warehouse of the Turks» was built in the 1200s. Its white façade and towers are reflected in the Grand Canal near San Stae.

Palazzo Loredan Vendramin Calergi. Designed by Mauro Coducci, it was begun in the late 1400s and finished in the early 1500s. Today the Palazzo is owned by the city of Venice and houses the winter Casino and its offices.

The Grand Canal seen from the Loggia ▶
delle Pescherie.

Palazzo Corner della Regina. So named because it occupies the site of the house in which Caterina Cornaro, Queen of Cyprus, was born in 1454, this palace was built in the mid-1700s yet clearly shows the influence of classical motifs.

The Fabbriche Nuove di Rialto. One of Sansovino's monumental albeit minor works, the building features a long arcade of white ashlar marble and double-tiered windows bordering the Grand Canal.

The Ca' d'Oro. This is the «house of gold», jewel of the Grand Canal with its polychrome stones, Gothic loggias that look like lace-work, and the arcade on the water evoking the mysteries of the Orient. Erected in the early 1400s, it could only have been by the hands of angels (Marino Contarini was the owner, Marco D'Amadio the architect and Matteo Reverti and Giovanni and Bartolomeo Bon the master builders).

Splendid, too, are the «calle» entrance (lane), the inner courtyard with its lace-like wall, the open stairway and the «vera» or well-cover.

From 1780 to 1784 it housed the Academy of Theatre called the «Ardenti». The villa and its art treasures were bequeathed to the state upon the death in 1922 of its owner, Baron Giorgio Franchetti (other owners included the Marcello, Loredan and Bressa families, Prince Trubetzkoi and Maria Taglioni, the famous ballerina).

Fontego dei Tedeschi. The «warehouse of the Germans» is a 16th-century building by Giorgio Spavento and Scarpagnino. Almost on the corner with the Rialto Bridge, it features a Renaissance façade and once boasted frescos by Giorgione (completely worn away by time). The side on the calle was frescoed by Titian. The inner courtyard is illuminated by an immense skylight and encircled by three tiers of galleries. In the middle is one of the omnipresent Venetian «vere» or well-covers.

Palazzo dei Camerlenghi. At one end of the Rialto Bridge where the «naranzeria» or orange market once stood is the austere, pentagonal Palace of the Chamberlains, the only Venetian edifice of more than four outer walls and each an authentic architectural gem in its own right. Built in the 16th century under Doge Andrea Gritti as the marble inscription on one of the façades on the Grand Canal attests, it was reputedly designed by Guglielmo Bergamasco. The upper floors once housed the revenue (three chamberlains) and other magistrates of the Venetian Republic and the ground floor the petty-crimes prison (the window bars can still be seen).

The Ponte di Rialto. The Rialto Bridge. Immortalised by photographers, poets, painters and songsters, it is one of Venice's main tourist attractions — as much a symbol of the city as the winged lion, the gondola, the Bridge of Sighs and St Mark's Bell Tower. Recently restored, the bridge has linked the banks of the Grand Canal for almost four centuries (since 1591), even today making the Rialto, with its markets, shops and public and private offices, the liveliest and most animated crossroads of the city.

Although said to have been designed by Giovanni Alvise Boldù, it may also have been planned in part by Antonio Da Ponte, who directed its building under Doge Pasquale Cicogna (as the inscriptions and emblems on the sides bear witness). The Rialto Bridge is 48 metres long and 22 wide, and its double-row shops joined in the middle by two arches sit on its single span over 28 metres long.

Majestically imposing yet softened by the graceful pair of balustrades, it features three flights of steps (on either side and in the middle) and the sculptural reliefs of the Dove, the Annunciation by Rubini and Tiziano Aspetti's St Mark and St Theodore adorning its sides.

Three years in the making, the present Ponte is the fourth to be er-

ected on the same site. The first, by Barattieri, was built of boats in 1181, the second, of wood on piles, in the mid-13th century, and the third, replacing the second after its collapse from the weight of a crowd gathered on it to see the Marchesa of Ferrara as she passed, a much larger wooden structure with a central draw-segment and shops in 1444. This bridge was never very

stable and, despite Spavento's repairs in 1501, the Venetian Republic decided to replace it with a stone one — the present bridge, first in the hearts of Venetians and famous the world over.

The Rialto's old wooden draw bridge for sail boats as it appeared in the late 15th century, detail from Vittore Carpaccio's painting «Relic of the True Cross Borne by the Patriarch of Grado, Francesco Querini, who Cures a Possessed Man» in the 20th room of the Galleria dell'Accademia.

Bathed in light, the Grand Canal winds past the San Samuele Bridge towards the Accademia flanked by an architectural display of rare beauty amid a palette of vibrant colours. Rising from the waters are Palazzo Moro in the style of Pietro Lombardo, the Gothic Palazzo Loredan called the Ambassador's Palace (15th century), the picturesque terrace of Casa Mainella, the classical lines of the Palazzi Contarini dagli Scrigni and Corfù, Mocenigo and Querini. Further ahead the Gallerie dell'Accademia delle Belle Arti (Gallery of the Fine Arts Academy), formerly the Scuola della Carità, is visible.

The Palazzi Loredan and Farsetti. Currently the seat of the municipal government and City Council, these two Palazzi are Venice's finest examples of the Veneto-Byzantine architectural style of the 1100-1200s.

Palazzo Grassi. This 18th-century patrician house is the work of G. Massari. It features frescos by A. Longhi and decorations by Guarana and Canal. Its reopening in 1986 following restoration was inaugurated by the Futurism show. It is used today to house art exhibits and theatrical performances.

Palazzo Balbi. «At the canal's bend». That's how Venetians tell you where the Palazzo is — right where the Grand Canal gently bends towards the Rialto on the right corner of Rio Novo. It was built by Nicolò Balbi, nobleman, upon his eviction from a previous residence for unremitted arrears. The architect was Alessandro Vittoria who, already under the Baroque influence, designed the house in the late 1500s. Napoleon Bonaparte watched the 1807 Regatta from its balconies.

45

The smaller of Cà Foscari's courtyards with its elegant stone stairway.

Ca' Foscari and Palazzo Giustinian. Were it not for their difference in size (Giustinian left, Foscari right), the two buildings might almost be twins as both feature Gothic façades. The first and second floors are accented by multi-light mullion windows with small balconies beneath, the top floors by four-light mullions and full windows on the ends. While the Giustinian's inner courtyard is a delight to behold that of Ca' Foscari is bare and pale in comparison, although its ornate entry gate in the wall with the Foscari coat-of-arms is noteworthy. Both of these Palazzi were built just after mid-century in the 1400s.

Ca' Rezzonico. Commissioned by the Priuli-Bon families in the mid-1600s, it is the work of Baldassare Longhena. The Palazzo or Ca' (literally house) was refurbished in 1752 by Massari for the Rezzonico family, a member of which was Pope Clement XIII. In the 1500s, Tiziano Vecellio (Titian) had his studio in the house formerly occupying this site. Although more delicately drawn to the discriminating observer, the façade echoes that of Ca' Pesaro as both were designed by Longhena.

The last private owner was the poet Browning (d. 1889), and, since 1935, it has been the seat of the Museo del Settecento Veneziano (Museum of the Venetian Settecento). This formidable art collection of the 1700s includes porcelain, ceramics, crystal, ornamental objects, lacquer and inlay furniture, frescos by Tiepolo, pastel works by Rosalba Carriera, sculptures by Vittoria, paintings by Guardi, bronze and silver works, the Murano «roses» or the famous Rezzonico chandeliers, sculpted fireplaces, a priceless spinet, «exam-

ples» of the printer's art of the period, a faithful reconstruction of the «Ai Due San Marchi» pharmacy that stood in Campo San Stin, a marionette theatre and other period pieces from the Republic's golden age.

Ca' Rezzonico's Brustolon Hall: This paragon of Venetian interior decor features furnishings by the celebrated intaglio master Andrea Brustolon.

Ca' Pesaro. Begun in the mid-1600s and completed in 1710, this Baroque palazzo was designed by Baldassare Longhena and built on the site previously occupied by a block of flats belonging to the Pesaro family. The cyclopean rustication of the «water-floor» features the two large portals and double-tiered rectangular windows and stands in vibrant contrast to the upper storeys with their full-length windows and columns reminiscent of Sansovino's Libreria di Piazza San Marco (St Mark's Square Bookshop). The rio side with its classical influences was designed by Antonio Gaspari, who also finished the work of the façade. The inner courtyard is noteworthy for its fine loggias and ornate well-cover or «vera» by Sansovino atop of which is Danese Cattaneo's Apollo.

In 1889, the Palazzo was bequeathed by countess Felicita Bevilacqua La Masa to Venice. The ornate rooms of the two middle storeys house the Gallery of Modern Art, the most interesting after Rome's and the one featuring the most works by foreign artists. The fourteen rooms of the third or top floor contain the important Oriental Art Museum collection.

«The Bishop». Purchased at the Venice Biennale of 1956, it is one of Giacomo Manzu's more important sculptures, Gallery of Modern Art, first floor, Ca' Pesaro.

48

Ippolito Caffi: Quay at Sunset (1864).

Luigi Nono: The Abandoned (1903).

Fioravanti Seibezzi: Self-Portrait (1929).

The Ponte dell'Accademia. With its weathered pattern of criss-crossed wooden beams, the Academy Bridge spans the Grand Canal from Campo San Vidal to Rio-terrà Antonio Foscarini and Campo della Carità next to the former Church of the Carità (current site of the Fine Arts Academy and Scuola Grande). Designed as a temporary structure in 1932 to replace the metal bridge built in 1854, it has «provisionally» endured, despite a 1933 project for a stone bridge by the late architect Torres as had been planned since the 15th century. After the Rialto and Scalzi Bridges, this is the third and last spanning the Grand Canal.

Ca' Venier dei Leoni. This short, white stump of a palazzo standing between the Accademia bridge and the Salute church presents a rather startling image with its towering courtyard trees. It is in fact the only part that was ever built of the stately mansion planned for this site by the Venier family in the mid-1700s (a wooden scale model by Lorenzo Boschetti is on display in the Correr Museum). Literally the «Venier House of Lions», the name supposedly refers to the owners pet lion which they kept in the garden.

The last private owner was Peggy Guggenheim, the American art collector, who bequeathed it to the city upon her death. Now a public

art gallery, it houses an important collection of modern art, including works by Picasso, Chagall, Ernst, Bracque, De Chirico and others, and a collection of primitive art.

Ca' Dario. To the right of the 15th-century, Gothic Palazzo Barbaro stands Palazzo Dario, with its superb polychrome façade adorned with ornate marble work and the typical Venetian beaker-like chimneys against the sky. Dating to the late 1400s, this Renaissance house was built for Giovanni Dario, the Venetian secretary at Constantinople. The design of this architectural gem is attributed to Pietro Lombardo and his school.

The splendid inner garden of the Guggenheim Museum in Ca' Venier dei Leoni and some of its sculptures by modern artists.

Ca' Pisani. This Renaissance-like building by Girolamo Frigimelica was built from the late 17th to the early 18th centuries. Comprising courtyards, tiered and overhanging loggias and two imposing façades, it presently houses the «Benedetto Marcello» Music Conservatory and Museum.

Palazzo Franchetti. Originally built in the 1400s, it was restored and considerably altered in 1890. The richly decorated window line in the centre of the façade is reminiscent of Palazzo Ducale's motifs.

La Salute. Literally «health», the name as well as the idea for this masterpiece of the Baroque stem from a vow made by the populace imploring the Virgin Mary to deliver Venice from an outbreak of the plague in 1630. In 1631 on the site of a temporary wooden church, Baldassari Longhena, commissioned by the Venetian Republic itself, began an undertaking that would span the next 50 years. He unfortunately died five years too soon and never saw its completion.

The Basilica is a majestic structure of gleaming white marble and azure-green cupolas or domes rising from an octagonal plan. The only break in the design is the flight of steps leading from the Basilica to the bank lapped to an emerald, velvet green by the waters and algae of the Grand Canal, here at its widest point looking towards St Mark's basin.

Santa Maria della Salute is immensely scenographic and complex. The octagon's sides (the rear one opens directly on to the presbytery) give rise to a façade of seven facets, six faces and the main façade. Each of the six faces features columns, niches, statues and a large three-light lunette. The main façade is monumental, reflecting Palladio's influence: tall co-

lumns interspersed with niches and statues, and a tympanum with balustrade supporting still more sculptures. It also acts as the frame for the imposing portal.

Culminating in the delicately wrought lantern crowned by the bronze statue of the Madonna, the vast dome appears as if buoyant, held in mid-air by the buttressing marble scrolls, each of which bearing the image of a saint. A smaller, rear dome is designed to endow the underlying presbytery with vertical amplitude. The two bell towers or campanili complete the profile.

Eight columns rise into the luminous interior, with each side featuring a chapel and altar. The far end holds the presbytery with transept and the high altar graced by the Greek icon of the Madonna Mora (Black Madonna). Brought to Venice from the island of Candia in 1672 by Francesco Morosini, it is the venerated Madonna della Salute.

Punta della Dogana. Looking like a ship's bow jutting seaward in St Mark's basin between the Grand and Giudecca Canals, Customs Point was a dock and storehouse for merchantmen in the days of the Republic. Built in 1675 by Bernardo Falcone, this vast triangular structure features columns, arcade and tower atop of which two Atlases balance a golden globe adorned by the revolving figure of Fortune.

The Gondola. Long, sleek, agile. Flat-bottomed, peculiarly awry yet graceful of line. The black swan— the world knows no equal—aglide with its metal bow «comb» and «curlicue» stern. The gondola. Proud, unique. The very symbol of Venice.

More than nine hundred years old, it has undergone many transformations since its first appearance. Only in the late 1700s did it assume its present form and substance.

Only a short time ago the building of a gondola demanded the finest woods available (modern

craftsmanship resorts to marine ply-wood). Oak planking, larch bottom boards, fir draught, cherry for the «trasti», linden for the inlay work, walnut oarlocks and beech oars.

The decorative bow iron or «comb» appeared in the 16th century, whereas the «felze» or carved wood cabin with its black curtain and ribbons, side windows and small two-wing door has disappeared but recently. Then, too, black has been the official colour— hull, «parecio» and adornments— from the 18th century, when the Venetian Senate deemed it necessary to put an end to the unbridled and spare-no-expense competition among the noble and wealthy to gad about in the most ornate, luxury-appointed and brilliantly coloured gondola. The gondola can be handled by either one oarsman or two, and includes two versions— the «casada» for the wealthy and il-

54

lustrious and the «parada» for everyday ferrying about.

The gondola has been an ever present inspiration to poets, writers, artists and photographers. And what better souvenir (bronze or glass, with or without the «carillon» or music box tinkling the famous tune of «La Biondina in Gondoleta») to remember your trip to Venice.

EXCURSION 3

Legend:

EXCURSION 4

Legend:

Excursion 3

GALLERIA DELL'ACCADEMIA - ZATTERE - CARMINI - SANTA MARIA DEI FRARI - S. ROCCO - CAMPO S. MARGHERITA - CAMPO S. POLO - CASA CENTANI - CAMPO S. GIACOMO DELL'ORIO - S. GIACOMETO - S. PANTALON

The Gallerie dell'Accademia. The city's most important museum, the Academy Galleries have been housed since 1750 in the 14th-century former Church of the Carità, the school of the Carità and the monastery of the Lateran Canons, this latter having been designed by Palladio.

The collections are laid out in twenty-four rooms, counting corridors and halls. The first contains anconas (altarpieces like the pala) and gilt on wood paintings by Lorenzo Veneziano, Nico di Pietro, Jacobello del Fiore and Michele Giambono; the second has works by Giovanni Bellini, Carpaccio, and Cima da Conegliano; one of the major paintings in the third room is the Madonna by Pordenone; in the fourth are the San Giorgio (St George) by Mantegna and Gianbellino's two Madonnas; in the fifth, Giorgione's «La Tempesta»; the sixth includes Bordone's masterpiece «La Consegna dell'anello al Doge» (Doge's ring ceremony) as well as works by Titian and Tintoretto; the seventh, Lotto's «Gentiluomo» (Gentleman) and paintings by Titian and Tintoretto; the rooms up to and including the eleventh contain works by Palma il Vecchio, Titian's «Pietà», Tintoretto's series of three canvases entitled «I Miracoli di San Marco» (Miracles of St Mark), Veronese's «Convito in Casa Levi» (Supper in the house of Levi) and Pordenone's vast pala «San Lorenzo Giustiniani».

Displayed in the next several rooms are works by 18th-century Venetian landscapists, by Schiavone and Bassano, and by 17th-century Italian artists and 18th-century Venetian painters. Giovan Battista Tiepolo's youthful works are found in the sixteenth room, while the following two offer 18th-century paintings, including Piazzetta's «Indovina» (Fortune-teller) and works by Guardi, Canaletto, Marco Ricci and Pietro Longhi. The next few rooms are dedicated to the paintings of the two Scuole (schools), San Giovanni Evangelista and Sant'Orsola, by Gentile Bellini and Carpaccio.

The next to last hall features Quattrocento and early Cinquecento art (1400s-1500s), including works by Vivarini Crivelli, Gentile Bellini and Cima da Conegliano. The last, once the Scuola della Carità's Albergo or lodgings, features Titian's «Presentazione della Vergine al Tempio» (Presentation of the Virgin in the Temple) and the triptych «Vergine con Putto e i Dottori della Chiesa» (Virgin with Putto and Doctors of the Church) by Antonio Vivarini and Giovanni d'Alemagna known as «da Muran».

Priceless light-blue and gold jewel-case. This room of the Academy Galleries is reserved for famous and rare art works.

Giovann Battista Piazzetta: L'Indovina (1740).

Francesco Guardi: Fire at S. Marcuola Oil Depot (1789).

Lorenzo Veneziani: Polyptych Lion (1375).

Canaletto (Giovan Antonio Canal): Capriccio (1765).

Tintoretto (Jacopo Robusti): S. Mark rescuing a slave (1548).

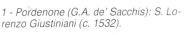

1 - Pordenone (G.A. de' Sacchis): S. Lorenzo Giustiniani (c. 1532).

2 - Giovanni Bellini: Vanitas (Prudence),
c. 1490.

3 - Jacopo Bellini: Madonna and Child
(1450-60).

4 - Giorgione: Tempest (c. 1506).

5 - Giorgione: La Vecchia (Old Woman),
1507-08.

Rio San Trovaso seen from where it ends at the Bridge of Marvels (Ponte de le meravegie). In the background is Casa Mainella and its large terrace with plants. Right: The base of the side faces of Palazzo Contarini degli Scrigni and Palazzo Corfù. The rio is well travelled as it connects the Giudecca and Grand Canals.

The Zattere. Panorama from the Giudecca Canal. Left: The buildings of the large shipping companies with their docks for cargo vessels and freighters and the long bridge over Rio San Trovaso. Centre: Adjoining the former friary is the Church of Santa Maria della Visitazione (Visitation) with its façade in the style of Pietro Lombardo and statue-adorned portal, the Artigianelli School of Arts and Crafts, and the Dominican Church of Santa Maria del Rosario (Rosary) called the «Gesuati».

The 14th-century portal with its Veneto-Byzantine ornamental motifs on the left side of the church.

The Zattere or «barges» are wide landings once used for barges laden with coal and timber. They were paved in 1519 and offer a splendid vista of Giudecca Island spread out before them. The Zattere stretch from the area known as Santa Marta to the Punta della Dogana (Customs Point).

The Carmini. Built in the 16th century on a site already occupied in the 12th and 13th centuries, the Church of the Carmelites features a distinctive three-face façade attributed to Sebastiano Lugano. The nave, its flanking columns with their ornate Byzantine capitals and two side aisles lend the interior a basilica-like aspect.

Historically, it once belonged to the Carmelite Order and featured an adjoining monastery which was demolished in 1810, leaving only the Renaissance cloisters. The church contains paintings by Cima da Conegliano, Lorenzo Lotto and Palma Giovane (the younger), the bronze bas-relief «La Deposi-zione» by Francesco di Giorgio Martini, and several frescos by Sebastiano Ricci.

The Scuola Grande dei Carmini is a late-Renaissance building attributed to Longhena. Formerly the seat of the Carmelite Confraternity founded in the late 1500s, it is famous for its Tiepolo paintings and Giovan Battista Piazzetta's «Judith and Holofernes», one of his most important works.

The church's basilica-like interior.

Santa Maria Gloriosa dei Frari. Begun in the mid-1100s on the site occupied by a church of the Order of Friars Minor (Franciscans), which was demolished at intervals as the present church took form, it was finally completed in 1443. In a style which may be termed monastery-Gothic, Santa Maria Gloriosa was supposedly designed by Nicolò da Pisa, although a more likely attribution would be to one Fra' Pacifico who is commemorated by a fine tombstone within.

Of brick as is the whole structure, the salient façade (partly protruding) features a magnificent portal adorned with three statues—those on either side are by Bartolomeo Bon and the central one by Alessandro Vittoria—and three beautiful rose windows. Full, finely fashioned Gothic windows provide the light for the apse and transepts.

Vast and luminous, the interior has a nave separated from the aisles on either side by double rows of stately columns. Six chapels branch off from the sides of the apse: to the left of which is the sacristy containing many famous art works. Behind the monumental high altar is Titian's masterpiece «L'Assunta» (Assumption). The presbytery includes the superb carved wood choir by Pietro Lombardo; the inlay work of the 124 stalls is by Cozzi. Many notables are also buried here: Titian, Canova and the Doges Nicolò Tron, Francesco Foscari and Giovanni Pesaro. The sculptures on each tomb are works of art in their own right. Along with the Church of SS Giovanni e Paolo, the Frari can also be considered a Venetian Pantheon.

Titian's celebrated altarpiece, «The Assumption».

The Choir. With its 124 stalls arranged in three tiers in the nave, it is an incomparable example of intaglio and inlay work of the 1400s.

San Rocco. Behind the Frari church in the «campo» (square) San Rocco is the church of the same name. Designed by Bon and originally erected in the late 1400s, it was rebuilt in 1725 by the architect Giovanni Scalfarotto, who was able to save the three original apses. The façade has a history of its own.

Fashioned into six panels the top and bottom of which on both sides adorned with niches containing the statues of the four Venetian saints, it was designed by Bernardino Maccaruzzi to the same proportions as the adjacent Scuola di San Rocco and built from 1765 to 1771. The unified nave interior features eight paintings by Tintoretto as well as works by Sebastiano Ricci and other artists. Tintoretto also decorated the organ's doors. The small bell tower dates to the 12th century.

To the right of the church stands the Scuola di San Rocco. With its imposing portal and Renaissance façade adorned with columns and paired windows, it is a fitting repository for the numerous works of art within.

Scuola Grande di San Rocco: The magnificent upper hall (salone superiore) with its 23 paintings by Tintoretto adorning walls and ceiling and 16th-century altar.

Campo San Polo (Paul). The city's largest «campo», San Polo takes you by surprise with its spaciousness, Venetian airiness and scenographic presence as you emerge from the narrow «calli» or lanes. Enclosed by stately palazzi and typical Venetian townhouses, including that of the geographer Adriano Balbi, the square takes its name from the church of the Apostle to the Gentiles that was built in the 9th century and completely reworked by Davide Rossi in 1884.

Campo Santa Margarita. Airy and always animated, this very popular campo lies between the Carmini church and San Pantalon. Adorned by two early 16th-century wells, it is bordered by typical 14th- and 16th-century houses. The most stately without doubt is the one built by the Celega brothers in the 1300s (they were the architect-builders of the Frari church's bell tower). Originally owned by the Foscolo family, it afterwards became the property of the Corners.

The Church of Santa Margarita, by which the campo is known, was first erected in the 9th century and then rebuilt in 1647. Few traces of it remain since it was turned into a cinema.

The Casa di Goldoni. Palazzo Centani is the official name of the house where Carlo Goldoni, the famous playwright, was born in 1707. It is one of the most typical of 15th-century Venetian town houses and boasts a beautiful inner courtyard with an open staircase gently terminating in a graceful curve. Casa Goldoni now houses the International Institute of Theatre Studies.

The Statue of Goldoni. Amid the people gathered in Campo San Bortolomio to exchange the day's «ciàcole» or small-talk stands in its bronze stillness Carlo Goldoni's likeness—a homage to 18th-century Venice's most native and wittiest son.

It is a tribute to the man whose genius took the simple, centuries-old «ciàcole», the birthright of every Venetian, and transformed it into art. Sculpted in 1883 by Antonio Dal Zotto, this Goldoni—with his ever-present pigeons dropping by or sitting on his tricorner hat—always has a good-natured smile for anyone who happens along or stops to chat in this «campo» encircled by typically Venetian houses. It's almost as if he were reminding his fellow townsfolk not to take the high water or the shortcomings of life in Venice too much to heart.

Campo San Giacomo dell'Orio (St James of the Laurel), with all of its trees and greenery, could almost be mistaken at first glance for a square in a small town. The church dates to the 9th century, when it was founded by Campoli da Oderzo and Muli dalle Contrade, and subsequently rebuilt in the 13th and refurbished in the 16th century. Together with its 12th-century square bell tower, it dominates most of the campo.

Next to the Ponte dell'Anatomia (Anatomy Bridge) is the building that housed the physicians' college founded in 1507.

San Giacometo. Legend and tradition have it that this small Church of St James at Rialto owes its construction to the vow of a carpenter in the wake of the famous fire that destroyed the Rialto's dwellings. Supposedly the oldest church in Venice, it dates from the 5th century AD and, despite the many refurbishings over the centuries, its original form is more or less intact.

«El Gobo» di Rialto. Sculpted in 1541 by Pietro di Salò, the «hunchback» of Rialto is an atlantes (male caryatid) supporting a proclamation stone, as the Latin inscription makes clear.

Church interior and ceiling painting, oil on canvas, San Pantalon in Glory, by G.A. Fumiani, 1643-1710.

Church of San Pantalon. Designed by Francesco Comino and built in 1686, it features a nave with vault ceiling and three lavishly decorated side chapels. The most famous of the paintings embellishing it is the ceiling's. Depicting scenes in the life of St Pantalon, it is the work of the Venetian artist Gian Antonio Fumiani, who is also buried in the church.

San Pantalon: Madonna and Putto in alabaster, 13th century.

69

Excursion 4

LA FENICE - PALAZZO DEL BOVOLO - SCUOLA & CHIESA DI S. FANTIN -
PINACOTECA QUIRINI/STAMPALIA - CAMPO SANTA MARIA FORMOSA -
SCUOLA DI S. MARCO - SANTI GIOVANNI & PAOLO - COLLEONI STATUE -
CHIESA DEI MIRACOLI - ABBAZIA & SCUOLA VECCHIA DELLA MISERI-
CORDIA - SANTA MARIA DELL'ORTO - GHETTO

La Fenice. With its imposing façade, Venice's pre-eminent theatre simply overpowers the small,
charming Campo San Fantin, with
its two ornate marble well-covers,
in which it stands. It also dominates
the 16th-century Church and Scuola della Buona Morte (the latter is
the seat of the city's university),
which are opposite and adjacent to
it, respectively.

Designed by Giannantonio Sel-
va and built in less than two years,

*La Fenice's auditorium, resplendent with
its stuccos and gilt intaglios.*

the Teatro La Fenice was inaugurated the evening of December the
26th, 1792. Following a fire in 1836,
it was restored to its original splendour (except for the façade) by the
brothers Giovanni Battista and
Tommaso Meduna.

With its pediment, tall columns
and steps, the façade awkwardly
mimics a typical Roman temple's.
Nonetheless, it has become a symbol to all music lovers. In the foyer
and atrium are portraits and statues of Goldoni (by Zandomen-
eghi), Rossini, Verdi and Wolf-Fer-
rari (this latter by Bertazzolo).

Sala della Spinetta (Spinet Room), one of the Apollonian rooms.

The theatre's main auditorium is a veritable jewel. Its exquisite elegance is everywhere enhanced by decorations, ornate stucco work, gold-leaf intaglios and panel paintings—on ceiling, in the boxes, along the corridors and about the orchestra. Decorations and stucco-work also adorn the foyer and other halls, which are often used for concerts and private parties. Of these rooms, the most beautiful and well appointed is the Apollinea, seat of the Philharmonic Society up to 1860.

The Scala del Bovolo. Built in the 15th century «of architectural excellence and at incredible expense», as the historian Martignoni states in the citation from Tassini, the Bovolo Stairs is one of the most famous of «hidden» Venice's curiosities. The spiral («bovolo» in Venetian dialect) flights were designed by the architect Giovanni Candi in marble and brick while the dome is lead. Restored in the 1600s, it adds the perfect finishing touch to the courtyard of Palazzo Contarini on Rio San Paterniano nearby Campo Manin.

Confraternities, the Scuola or school housed the Venetian Society of Medicine. Today it is the seat of the University of Venice and its fine library.

A Crucifixion by Andrea Dell'Aquila adorns the façade below the open-base pediment's apex, and his Madonna and Rubini's angels stand on its top and sides.

On the ground floor inside the Scuola are works by Tintoretto, Paolo Veronese and Vittoria, and Palma Giovane (the Younger) painted the ceiling's thirteen coffers. An imposing staircase leads to the top floor and the room called Saletta Tommaseo with its wealth of decorations and paintings.

The Scuola di San Fantin. Damaged by fire, it was rebuilt in a style mixing the classical and Baroque by Antonio Contino in the late 1600s. It was originally the seat of the Confraternities of St Jerome and Santa Maria della Giustizia or della Buona Morte (Justice or the Good Death), so called because the brethren aided and comforted those condemned to death. In 1811, following the banning of the

The Querini-Stampalia Biblioteca and Pinacoteca. In a small square or «campiello» lapped by water on two sides and located behind the Church of Santa Maria Formosa stands the Palazzo Querini-Stampalia, just beyond several beautiful houses. It houses the library and art collection or gallery of the family Foundation, established by the bequest of Count Giovanni Querini-Stampalia in 1868.

The library is on the first floor. The gallery, which occupies the palazzo's largest room, boasts

The «Aula Magna» or conference hall of the university. Restored in 1913, it was once the Scuola's oratory.

One of the second-floor rooms of the Querini-Stampalia Gallery with Sebastiano Ricci's «Three Allegories of Day» on the ceiling. It also boasts one of the collection's masterpieces, «Judith Holding Holofernes' Head» by Vincenzo Catena (16th century).

18th-century furnishings and early 17th-century sculptures and globes.

Campo Santa Maria Formosa. Named for the church which unevenly divides it in two, with each part having its own well-cover and scenic palazzi, this «campo» or square is another focal point of animated city life, beginning each day with the opening of the local market's stalls. Originally erected in the 7th century AD under the bishop San Magno di Oderzo, the church was rebuilt in 1492 by Mauro Coducci. It has two façades: one, giving on the nearby canal, was erected in 1542 to honour Vincenzo Cappello (whose statue is visible), victorious over the Turks: and the other, facing the square, was completed in 1604. This latter is adorned by three busts of members of the Cappello family (who funded its building) and five statues—the Madonna and the Virtues.

Of Latin-cross plan, the church houses important art works by Bartolomeo Vivarini, Palma Giovane (Younger) and Palma Vecchio (Elder). Between the church and the 1611 Baroque bell tower with its fine mascaron (decorative grotesque head) is the oratory which contains Tiepolo's Madonna con Putto e San Domenico (Madonna with Putto and St Dominic).

The Scuola di San Marco. Founded in the latter half of the 12th century for humanitarian purposes, the Scuola Grande di San Marco or «dei battuti» (downtrodden) was designed in the main by Pietro Lombardo and Buora and built following the 1485 fire that destroyed the original building. The top of the façade and the large interior staircase are by Coducci, while Sansovino was responsible for the subsequent addition and completion works on the Scuola's Rio Mendicanti side. The façade facing the campo or square and next to the Church of Santi Giovanni e Paolo features a fine portal with two dancing putti on the flanking basework, a large lunette with marble statues of St Mark, the Confraternity brethren and, just above them, Charity. The four marble reliefs also flanking the portal depict two lions in perspective and two episodes from St Mark's life.

The upper half of the façade recalls the motifs of the golden Basilica itself. The interior, which today houses the city's public hospitals group, comprises an immense ground-floor hall with double rows of columns and exposed beam ceiling, and, on the upper floor, a large hall once used for public gatherings with an altar by Sansovino and paintings by minor artists and the room called the «Sala dell'Albergo» containing an intaglio ceiling with decorations, and paintings by Palma Vecchio (Elder) and by the school of Gianbellino.

tributed to the school of Gambello and Bon, is Renaissance Gothic. The sarcophagi of Jacopo and Lorenzo Tiepolo, Daniele Bon and Marco Michiel are found at the base of the façade.

Venice's Pantheon. Supposedly armed with Nicolò da Pisa's plans, two monks built this church on what had been marshland when it was donated to the Dominicans in 1234 by Doge Jacopo Tiepolo. Together with the Frari church, it is one of the longest in Italy.

The Pantheon is Venetian-Gothic in style, while the main portal, at-

In the right stilted blind arch is the funerary sculpture of Doge Michele Steno (d. 1413) found in the left aisle of the Church of Santi Giovanni e Paolo. The marble figure of the Doge, depicted lying on an urn, was part of the original monument fashioned in the style of the 14th century found in the Church of Santa Marina. Under the left arch is the marble figure of Alvise Trevisan, author. On either side of the blind arches stand the statues of St Peter Martyr (right) and St Thomas Aquinas dating to the early 16th century.

The Latin-cross interior features a nave and flanking aisles, ten imposing supporting columns, splendid mullion apse windows, and a

magnificent 15th-century Murano stained-glass window with figures on the transept's righthand wall.

Historically, the funerals of the doges were held here, and it is called the Pantheon della Serenissima because it contains the tombs of and memorial works to many of the Republic of St Mark's famous notables.

The Colleoni. The mounted bronze figure of Bartolomeo Colleoni, for twenty years the most feared yet most fascinating mercenary in the service of the Venetian Republic during the 15th century, stands proudly between the Church of Santi Giovanni e Paolo and a row of typical townhouses. Andrea del Verrocchio took seven years to complete it in 1488, and Alessandro Leopardi cast it in 1496. It is a masterpiece of Renaissance sculpture. One curious note. Colleoni, who donated part of his estate to Venice, left instructions that the statue was to be placed in Piazza San Marco.

The Chiesa dei Miracoli. Built from 1481 to 1489, the Church of St Mary of Miracles was designed by Pietro Lombardo and is considered his masterpiece. The exterior, with its strange rust-coloured marble panelling, is a fascinating blend of Veneto-Byzantine and Renaissance styles. The interior features a tunnel-vaulted nave ending in a stairway leading to the presbytery. The overhead choir is also quite impressive.

Tradition has it that Santa Maria dei Miracoli was built with the offerings people made to a centuries-old miracle-working icon of the Madonna, which a man named Amadi kept in the courtyard of his house. Now in the church, the icon is still venerated today.

Rio dei Miracoli, one of Venice's most charming rios with the long arcades of the houses on the water. In the background is the Widman Bridge, so called for a group of wealthy merchants from Carinthia who lived in a nearby palazzo designed by Longhena.

The Scuola and Abbazia della Misericordia. This is the school-abbey complex of the Brothers of Mercy. It was built next to the 10th-century Church of Santa Maria called «Valverde» or green glen as it stands on the island of the same name that was once covered with gardens and meadows. The confraternity's original seat was the 15th-century Scuola Vecchia (old) and was later moved to the Scuola Nuova (new) built in 1534 by Sansovino, who left it unfinished.

Time and the vagaries of fortune have left very little art work: two angels on the architrave of the Scuola Vecchia's façade and traces of the ornate interior decorations in the hall on its first floor. The Scuola Nuova's vast halls retain, too, only traces of frescos and ornamentation.

Adjacent to the Scuola Vecchia is a small, charming Gothic clois-ters. The remains of an extremely long arcade or portico, once part of the vast hall, are to be seen on the foundations.

The Scuola Vecchia and Abbazia della Misericordia at Cannaregio.

Tintoretto is buried in one. The façade boasts a fine rose window, two four-light mullion windows on either side, and an ornate marble portal over which are the statues of St Christopher, the Virgin and the Archangel Gabriel. The two sloping side roofs are crowned by the figures of the 12 apostles sculpted by the Delle Masegne brothers. Also noteworthy are the five canopied spires and the imposing domed bell tower.

The most important art works on display inside are Jacopo Tintoretto's «Adoration of the Calf» and «Last Judgement», Palma Giovane's «God the Father in Glory» and «Annunciation», Cima da Conegliano's pala or altarpiece «St John the Baptist and Saints» and Vittoria's sculptures.

The Ghetto. The Ghetto—both old and new parts—is strikingly picturesque, with its tall narrow-windowed houses, shops, synagogues and wells occupying a charming area of the Sestiere di Cannaregio district near San Ger-

The Madonna dell'Orto. Literally the Madonna of the Garden, it was so named because it houses a miraculous picture of the Virgin which was found in a nearby garden. The church features a nave and side aisles with apse chapels—

The «squero» or shipyard at Madonna dell'Orto.

The Ghetto's Campo and the characteristically tall Jewish houses.

olamo. It was here that the Jews from Giudecca Island and the other areas of the Republic were transferred by Senate decree in 1516. Here, too, is where the name itself, unfortunately adopted elsewhere to designate the place where the Jews were and are forced to live, originated. Historically, the area was once set aside for the foundries that cast metals and made bombards or mortars. In Italian the word for casting is «getto», whence ghetto.

The Ghetto has six synagogues, also called Schola (from the Greek). There are the German-rite Schola, built in 1526 and featuring tapestries, beautiful sacred vestments and ornaments and a Sefertic containing the scroll of the Law; the unadorned 1529 Canton Schola; the italian Schola, erected in the late 1500s; the Levantine-rite Schola with its superb portal; the Luzzato Oratory of the 1600s noted for the beautiful intaglio work in its upper room; and the Spanish-rite Schola, rebuilt in 1635 and attributed as the work of Baldassare Longhena.

The recently restored Levantine-rite Schola synagogue (1538). Opposite is the Spanish Schola by Longhena.

Jewish shop with sign in one of the Ghetto's lanes.

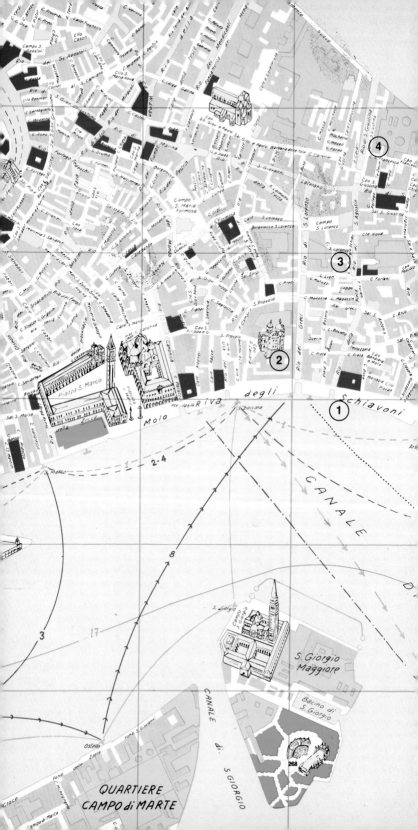

EXCURSION 5

Legend:

Riva degli Schiavoni: Panorama

Excursion 5

(map pp. 80-81)

RIVA DEGLI SCHIAVONI - S. ZACCARIA - SCUOLA S. GIORGIO DEGLI SCHIAVONI - S. FRANCESCO DELLA VIGNA - MUSEO STORICO NAVALE - ARSENALE - GIARDINI & BIENNALE

Riva degli Schiavoni. From Piazza San Marco one crosses the Ponte dei Sospiri and the Ponte della Paglia (straw bridge) until coming upon the wide vista of the basin. It's a fine stroll from here to the gardens, with the way elegantly appointed by luxury hotels and popular, fashionable in-spots. The Riva (bank) gets its name from the Dalmatian seamen (Schiavonia) whose ships once docked here.

The Church of San Zaccaria. The final resting place of eight doges, St Zachary's is built on the remains of an earlier church (9th-11th centuries) of which only the crypt under San Tarasio's chapel and part of the left aisle are left. The 15th-century façade is the work of Gambello and Coducci. The lower half with the reliefs of the Prophets is by the former: the rest is by the latter. On the portal is Vittoria's statue of St Zachary, whose tomb inside was partly sculpted by the same artist.

In addition to Giambellino's

masterpiece «The Madonna and Child Enthroned and Saints», the other works include those by Tintoretto, Van Dyck, Palma Giovane, Palma Vecchio and Vivarini. Also noteworthy are the hanging urn by Marco Sanudo, the Coro delle Monache (Nuns' Choir), and the five, splendid 18th-century gilt armchairs reserved for the doge and his retinue.

Inside view with the high-altar

Giovanni Bellini: Sacra Conversazione.

Chapel of St. Tarasio: affreschi di A. del Castagno 1462

The 16th-century, ground-floor hall with its exposed-beam ceiling where the School's celebrated cycle of paintings by Carpaccio can be seen.

The Scuola di San Giorgio degli Schiavoni.

St George's School was built by the Dalmatians (Slavs whence Schiavoni), once quite numerous in Venice, to accommodate their religious and community assemblies. It is not far from the Church of St John Templar of the Knights of Malta and the small campo where the house of Ugo Foscolo, one of the greatest poets of the Italian Renaissance, is found. The School's artistic and historical integrity is preserved intact. The façade, designed by Giovanni De Zan in the early 1500s, incorporates motifs made famous by Sansovino.

San Francesco della Vigna.

Occupying a former vineyard (vigna), the church was designed by Sansovino and completed in time to accommodate Andrea Palladio's façade. The interior's many chapels, some of which bearing the names of noble Venetian families, are well deserving of a visit. The fine wooden high altar is attributed to Longhena. The nave, transept and chapels boast numerous fine works of art by, among others, Vivarini, Vittoria, Paolo Veronese, Frà Antonio da Negroponte, Pietro Lombardo, Giambellino, Tiepolo, Palma Giovane, Titian and Aspetti. Famous, too, is the icon of the Madonna called «Celestia». It once belonged to the now demolished church-convent of Madonna Celeste, which also gave its name to the popular nearby neighbourhood.

84

The Naval Museum: Adjacent to the Church of San Biagio or Blaise, rebuilt in the 1700s, where Angelo Emo, the last Venetian commander who led a fleet against the Tunisians, is buried.

The Museo Storico Navale.

The Naval History Museum has been housed in an imposing 16th-century building, once the Republic's granary, next to St Blaise's church since 1964. Though officially set up in 1919, the museum contains collections far older — most of its models come from the Arsenale collections dating to the late 1600s. On the ground floor are seven Venetian cannons from Famagusta (Cyprus) and Candia and the marble likeness of Angelo Emo by Antonio Canova. The Bucintoro is among the museum's most prized models.

The second floor houses the ships of the Italian Navy from 1860 to the present, arranged as if passing in review. On the third floor is to be found a rare collection of 28 model Chinese and Far-eastern junks, generous gift of a French collector. Noteworthy items in the other rooms include an authentic 18th-century galiot (perhaps Maltese), 70 seamen's «ex voto», numerous models of lagoon craft, and gondolas with their fittings (pareci), irons (ferri) and cabins (felze).

Late 17th-century wood sculpture depicting a Turk chained to the rigging.

85

The Arsenale gates or «porte» with the wooden bridge spanning the Rio Galeazze.

The Lion of Piraeus that once adorned a fountain in the Greek port city. The symbols and words it bears were deciphered in 1856 by the Danish scholar Rafn. They were carved by Scandinavian mercenaries called «Veringhi» during the repression after a revolt in Piraeus. Not visible in the photo is the other lion, in prone position, that was once a monument on the road from Athens to Eleusis.

The Arsenale.

For Venice, Mistress of the Seas, nothing but the largest of shipyards would do—the Arsenale. It was built by order of Doge Ordelaffo Valier in 1104 on the «gemelle» or twin islands on the city's northern outskirts. From it sallied forth the fleets of galleys, driven as much by oar and sail as by the Venetians' dreams of conquest, that would carry the ensign of St Mark to the farthest reaches of the Levant. Girded by walls and guarded by towers, additions and expansion were commonplace during the halcyon days of Venetian power: 1303-1325 enlarged, 1473 new galley yards, 1539 large new dockyard for galliasses, 1574 the Sanmicheli dockyard for the Bucintoro, 1579 the Tana or ropeworks was built by Antonio Da Ponte with its three enormous aisles laid out for the manufacture and storage of rigging, and thereafter Scalfarotto's workshops and annexed stores and sail loft.

The Arsenale was run by three Procurators or superintendents. The initial labour force of 1000 «arsenalotti» or workers, fulcrum

The towering cranes and scaffolding of the Arsenale's drydocks seen from the lagoon. Right foreground: Fishing nets in the water.

and often the mainstay of the citizenry's freedom, was to number 16,000 at the height of Venice's economic and political empire. Today as still and pulseless as the memories of past glory it evokes, the Arsenale no longer answers to Dante's description «Fore and aft the hammers wield, they the oars others the rigging make, there the reefs to patch here the keel...».

Flanked by the lions from Greece that Francesco Morosini brought back in 1687, Antonio Gambello's monumental land entrance also features the statues of Neptune, the goddess Bellona, Justice, Vigilance, Abundance and Mars as well as two mysterious figures of unknown identity. Rio Galeazze flows between the towers providing the boat access.

Gambello's entrance and its marble memorials to the Battles of Lepanto and Morea.

The Gardens and Biennale.

The gardens cover the vast «Castello» area formerly occupied by the Zitelle Conservatory, St Dominic's church and monastery, St Anthony Abbot's church and monastery, St Nicolò of Bari's church and the seamen's hospital. Napoleon had them razed to make way for trees and gardens similar to Paris'.

Viale Garibaldi is the avenue that runs from the Gardens' main entrance to the Via or street of the same name (at Rioterrà) from which it is closed off by tall gates.

Opposite these is a statue in bronze of Garibaldi «Hero of Two Worlds». Running east from the bridge, the Gardens branch out beyond Viale Trieste and along the Basin as far as the avenue leading into the Biennale's grounds. Apart from the exhibition pavilions, the grounds themselves are the most beautiful part of the Gardens, featuring knolls, paths and wooded areas. The park is also dotted with many monuments to the famous and notable.

The Biennale d'Arte is the international art expo held here every two years. Begun in 1895, it gathers and displays works from Italy and participating nations from all over the world.

The Rumanian Pavilion.

88

Excursion 6

THE LAGOON ISLANDS

Giudecca. The «fondamenta» or quayside of Santa Croce and Zitelle seen from the Church of the Redentore's (Redeemer) campo. Background: The Zitelle Church (left) with its tympanum façade, two flanking bell towers and great dome. Foreground: The «bricole», groups of 3-4 mooring piers linked together in the water for the docking of large vessels.

Once called «Spinalonga» for its herring-bone shape, Giudecca Island probably derived its name from the fact that many Jews (Giudei in Italian) once lived there. Another version disputes this and would have the name come from the fact that certain properties on the island were once «giudicati» or assigned to certain noble families who had been given permission to return from exile.

San Zorzi (San Giorgio Maggiore).
After more than a century of being abandoned, the island has once again come to life. The revival is due to Count Cini and the Foundation that bears the name of his son, Giorgio, who died in a plane accident in 1951. It attracts scholars, artists and scientists the world over to its School of Venetian Studies. Through cultural exchanges and social activities, it promotes research in the fields of art, literature, music and theatre, having become in the process a spiritual beacon for modern man.

The church is by Palladio and the façade, with its marble figures of the Doges Tribuno Memmo and Sebastiano Ziani by Giulio del Moro, resembles that of the Church of the Redentore (Redeemer).

The island of San Giorgio Maggiore, seat of the Cini Foundation, seen from the former royal gardens (giardini reali).

The Lido.
That inviting expanse or «foulard» of greenery and sand, the Lido remains even today one of the most fashionable of international seaside resorts and one of the world's most renowned beaches, despite the weakening of the tourist boom over the last few years. Set between the sea and the lagoon as if protecting Venice, the Lido is eleven kilometres long and only a few hundred metres wide in certain place. One end faces Punta Sabbioni on the mainland and the other Santa Maria del Mare on the island of Pellestrina. The «bocche» or harbour openings separate it from both. It has only been within the last century that the Lido, thanks to both private and public initiatives (led by Ettore Sorger), has become a residential and resort area. Where once only dunes and tracts of wilderness existed, today there are populous developments such as Città Giardino, Ca' Bianca and Alberoni.

Apart from its beaches, the Lido is also noted for its casino, internationally famous golf links and the international Mostra del Cinema or Film Festival.

Torcello. Beyond the marshes where the seagulls nest among the dry and salt-sprayed grasses, Torcello's cathedral and its bell tower are silhouetted against a crystal-clear sky. Surrounded by Santa Fosca and a few other unyielding vestiges of former glory, these are the last witnesses of the island's once thriving and prosperous community, destroyed by the sea and the advancing swamp.

Murano. Amurianum as it was called in antiquity, Murano too was settled by people seeking refuge from the advancing barbarians. It was always protected by the Serenissima and its inhabitants were granted special privileges and political rights. By virtue of its glassworks, it soon became a veritable city with its own upper and lower house town assemblies, doge's representative and register of first

families. It is located in the northern part of the lagoon beyond San Michele Island and can be seen from Venice's Fondamenta Nuove (new quayside).

Boasting a plethora of palazzi, churches, monasteries, parks and even vegetable gardens, Murano basked in the radiance of Venice, sharing then as now its fortunes.

One phase of the glass-blowing process.

The Basilica di Santa Maria e San Donato.

This is a prime example of the successful blending of Byzantine and Lombard styles in Venetian architecture. Endowed with a Latin-cross plan but without a dome, the Basilica was founded in the 7th century, rebuilt about 1140 and subsequently restored.

Burano.

Like Murano and Torcello, Burano too was populated by people fleeing the onslaught of the barbarian invaders. It actually comprises four small islets linked by stone and wooden bridges.

Aereal view of Burano

Conc. S.M.A. 207/68 Fotocolor Fot. 09577

Feast of the Redeemer. The «Festa del Redentore» is Venice's most extravagant and popular holiday. It falls on the third Saturday and Sunday of July and attracts both Venetians and visitors from all over the world.

The festivities begin with religious services in the Church di Gesù Redentore (Christ Redeemer). An imposing white edifice designed by Palladio, it stands in the middle of Giudecca Island as a symbol of thanksgiving for deliverance from the plague of 1576. A temporary yet picturesque bridge of boats is thrown across the Giudecca Canal to accommodate the faithful who gather on the quayside for the procession that punctually opens the ceremonies.

The Regatta's Pageantry. A vivid, centuries-old tradition, the Regata Storica is revived annually on the first Sunday afternoon of September when the brilliant costumes and fittings of both oarsmen and boats glide down the Grand Canal in stunning pageantry.

Venice's most important spectacle in terms of its popular appeal

and folklore, the race marked its 684th running in 1986, drawing more Venetians and visitors from abroad than any other event in the city's calendar of special occasions. The Regatta brings out the best in Venice, where even the palazzi and houses are bedecked with tapestries, carpets and flags, thus becoming an incomparable backdrop to the throngs of viewers enthusiastically crowding the quaysides, banks, ferries and squares along the route.

The Palio. First organised in 1955 by the tourism boards and other city agencies of the four cities involved, the Palio delle Repubbliche Marinare is held every four years in Venice. It is a race commemorating the power and glory of the four great maritime republics — Venice, Genoa, Pisa and Amalfi.

Each city is represented by its galleons bearing the appropriate symbol: the winged-horse of Amalfi, the dragon of Genoa, the lion of Venice and the eagle of Pisa. Each boat, a faithful replica of an original, weighs 800 kilos and is powered by eight oarsmen.

A colourful parade, with participants lavishly dressed in period costumes, sets the atmosphere and introduces the Palio. As the parade files its way from the Palazzo Ducale's courtyard and across St Mark's Square to the Molo or quayside, it is followed by thousands of spectators who applaud the «figuranti» or costumed representatives of the four cities as they pass.

Carnival. A tradition returns. The need for peace and quiet; a chance to get to know one another, a party in the family of man. In this most Universal of cities, Venice has revived the deepest and most popular meaning in human terms as well as a tradition.

CONTENTS

Testi a cura di: L. Castro
Foto: Barone - Firenze
A. Costantini
F. Frassinetti
F. Roiter - Arch. Ed. Zerella - Venezia

editions **ITALCARDS**
bologna - italy
© copyright reserved
LA FOTOMETALGRAFICA EMILIANA S.p.A.
S. Lazzaro di Savena - Bologna - Italy
Reproduction, even partial, forbidden

Finished printing in june 1988

Edizioni Zerella - Venezia
S. Marco 3576 - Tel. 041/5205797